Our God Reigns
Inspirational Prophetic Christian Poetry

Volume 3

Deborah Esther Nyamekye

ISBN: 978-1-9163509-4-6

DEDICATION

I dedicate this book to the Holy Spirit of God the Creator and Father who came to earth in the person of my Lord and Saviour Jesus Christ. Words cannot express the depth of my gratitude for the Holy Spirit's faithfulness in transforming my life and empowering me.

The Holy Spirit has also painstakingly taught me to partner wholeheartedly with God and in so doing I have over the years experienced deliverance and healing as well as fulfillment of prophetic destiny in a way I would never have imagined. An example is the mandate to write for the glory of God which in so doing birthed these volumes of poetry books among others.

Our God Reigns! Let the Earth Rejoice!

CONTENTS

Hear the LORD, Awake!

Zechariah, the priest prophesied to his son John
"And you, my little son, will be called the prophet of
the Most High, because you will prepare the way for the Lord.
You will tell his people how to find salvation
through forgiveness of their sins. Because of God's tender mercy,
the morning light from heaven is about to break upon us,
to give light to those who sit in darkness and in the shadow of
death and to guide us to the path of peace[1]."

LORD may your people hear your voice speaking loud and
clear to us, the call of each one as the call to John the Baptist,
who said "I am a voice shouting in the wilderness,
Clear the way for the LORD's coming!'"

Oh merciful Father speak loud! Raise your voice as a trumpet
sound over the nations, to the saints anointed to tell
people how to find salvation through forgiveness of their
sins and chosen to tell people of Jesus,
"the only Way, Truth and Life", the Way to eternal life.
Raise your voice, LORD!

Awake! Awake! Saints, respond to the light of His countenance
as the morning light from heaven breaking forth upon us.
Do His bidding as the light of the world set on a hill for
all to take refuge and find healing. Be a friend to the lonely and
broken hearted, offer a lamp to their feet and a light unto their
pathway, that they may know God and be carried on
the wings of His peace out of the abyss of death and

into His heavenly realm of eternal life.
Awake! Awake! SAINTS.

Scriptural inspiration: John 14:6-7, John 1:23/Is 40:3, Matt. 5:14,
Psalm 119:105, Quote 1: Luke 1:76-79 NLT.

The Battle is the LORD's ! (Poetic Song)

The Battle is the LORD's
I shall declare it, far and near
and shall not fear.

The Battle is the LORD's yet
He arms me with strength.
I march in awe.
Encouraged and bonded with
soldiers, we march in awe.

Our strength is in
weapons from above,
mighty to pull down every
stronghold, and cast down all
powers binding people of God.

The Battle is the LORD's
I shall declare it,

far and near and shall not fear.

The Battle is the LORD's yet
He gives me strategies.
I march to war.
Skilled and schooled with
generals, we march to war.

Our strategies are wisdom
from God above,
Mighty to pull down every
high thing, and cast down all exalted
against the knowledge of God.

We are one, from every nation,
regardless of race, association,
rich or poor and life's station
He calls us, we are one,
and He arms us as one.

The Battle is the LORD's
We shall declare it, far and near
and shall not fear. We shall not
fear for the battle is the LORD's!

Scriptural inspiration:
John 17:21, 2 Corinth. 10:5, 2 Corinth. 10:4, 2 Chronicles 20

———— ** ————

Intimacy & Destiny Restored (Poetic Song)

Introduction:
Testimony is powerful in the life of the Christian in that it serves to reveal how God has worked in their lives. It therefore gives glory to God, strengthens the faith of hearers and could be a means to draw unbelievers to Christ resulting in their Salvation. Let's keep up with the testimonies whether verbal or written in the form of an article, a song set to music or a poem. This joyful believer in Christ has chosen

to write a poem to sing unto the Lord regarding His goodness in restoring them back to a life of intimacy and a destiny in service to God.

I will sing of the goodness of the LORD!
For He has restored blessings lost.
As a child I hold his hand and skip along
with a face beaming at the thought of
His plans ahead and His goodies galore.

As a dancer I glide with ease to and fro only trained by the
Spirit's flow, filled with joy at every step and twirl as my body
sways and receives God's healing thrill.

As an intercessor I pray God's will on my knees or as I sit,
stand and lay me down, a trainee of the Spirit who is taught
so well. I enter spiritual realms few tread with the
Spirit at the head proclaiming "liberty!" while breaking yokes
and releasing captives in this time of Jubilee.

As a witness, I am a love letter God writes to the world saying
"Come to me, return to the fold and be made whole".
I am a light-bearer to showcase the truth of my Master's Word for
therein can be found the Light of the World,
Jesus Christ.

His Light within sets me ablaze to recount reams of God's
deeds and to expose the trickster's schemes at a count of 1,2,3.

As an overcomer in jubilation,
I proclaim "Gracious God, all my life,
I "will give a testimony of your great goodness and will joyfully
sing of Your righteousness[1]""

Quote (1) Psalm 145:7 HCSB

———————— *** ————————

Fruitful & Free

Peace like a river.
Light as a feather.
Whatever the weather,
gliding through life,
shielded from strife.
Fruit bearing & ripe
as a branch in the
blessed vine.

Scriptural inspiration: John 15

Ability to be a Somebody
**

A nobody can become a somebody someday.
If not today or tomorrow it shall be one day, 'cause
everybody has the ability. It is possible if you do not loose
focus or direction but set your sights on your vision,
based on wisdom from the book of instruction.

Use the key of divine knowledge to open doors.
Advance at the beat of the sound of your vision calling.
The pace is set by the rhythm of the songs of your heart responding.

The blessed vision is a reflection of the somebody you have aimed
to be beckoning as from the sky,
full of wisdom and knowledge of the Most High.

In the ascent to be a somebody, joys and trials are for your
wrapping as a gift of integrity.
Be a somebody today to help a nobody find their way some day.

—————— ** ——————

The Most High's Voice - Greatest Sound of All!
(Ref. Psalm 29)

Most High, talking, chirping, mooing and barking
are sounds that we hear from some of your creatures great
and small.

When we hear the sound of the gusts of wind, drops of rain,
hooting cars, the screeching train and the cracking violent sound of
thunder from the sky, it's the daily melody of Your created earth.

When we hear the sound of the rise and fall of spluttering waves,
the ship docking and berthing, sea gulls wailing and squawking, it's
the mixture of stillness and squalling of
the coastal shores you created.

God, none of these sounds have the power to change
lives as your mighty voice, nor match the sound of
your soothing words of comfort when we seek your fortitude.

There is no sound on earth greater than your voice that is
…over the waters;
The God of glory thunders;
The LORD *is* over many waters.
[4] The voice of the LORD *is* powerful;
The voice of the LORD *is* full of majesty.
[5] The voice of the LORD breaks the cedars,
Yes, the LORD splinters the cedars of Lebanon
…in His temple everyone says, "Glory!"[1]

So, to you we ascribe all our worship, declaring:
"The LORD sat *enthroned* at the Flood,
And the LORD sits as King forever.
[11] The LORD will give strength to His people;
The LORD will bless His people with peace."[2]

Quotes: (1) Psalm 29:3-5, 9 NKJV (2) Psalm 29:10-11 NKJV

________________ *** ________________

Get Ready, the Bridegroom Cometh!

I believe in Jesus Christ. He is the Son of God.
A Son unlike any other who left his throne to
became as you and I. Walking among a crowd, he healed,
taught and mended broken lives. Many believed, some doubted,
but he stopped not his mandate for mankind.

Have you ever heard of a Son such as this, a man of this kind?
Have you seen one so pure and true? One who is impartial and
kind. A lover of all; rich, poor, the Jew and gentile?

He finished his work when he died and ascended to his throne.
Now seated, the King makes intercession for co-heirs now and
those to come. Are you on a risky tightrope between heaven and hell
with your gaze set on that place where sorrow untold with
everlasting chains awaits? Or are you ready for
the Bridegroom when he comes?

As a bright lamp full of oil, keep your soul ready and ablaze.
There is still time to prepare for the King,
so live not in uncertainty or in a maze.

Scriptural inspiration: Matthew 25

———————— ** ————————

His Excellency

Why mourn what was not but could have been,
what is the point as it never was, nor will it be?
Yesterday God planned,
today He has in hand
and tomorrow God will certainly man!

Who can judge God's might?
An omnipotent, omniscient and
omnipresent God is He.

Why reject your body and weight?
You see ugly, your potter sees beautiful.
You see old and haggard, your redeemer sees youth renewed.

Why regret your nation and culture?
You see primitive, your Master sees unique.

Why be ashamed of yourself and status?
You see poor, your maker sees rich.
Your worth is not in your wealth or know-how
comparable to another.

Who can question God's excellence?
A skilled creator no one can deny.

___________ ** ___________

Whose Report Shall We Believe?
**

Whose report shall we believe?
The Lord's freedom report of the kingdom child.

His report says we are freely his
and free to be as he is.

His report says we bear his Cross.
A love bridge from gloom to glory for those regarded as dross.

Not ashamed we broadcast our views as Breaking News.
Out of the "rubbish bin",
we are cherished kinsmen of Christ the King.

Beautiful Feet
*

Light of the world,
overcame darkness
in my life and paths
of strife.

My feet, he released
from mire and took
me up for repair.

Now set on a hill,
a restorer of the breach
on life's treadmill with
beautiful feet,
the lost to reach.

Scriptural inspiration:
How beautiful on the mountains are the feet of the messenger who
brings good news, the good news of peace and salvation, the news that the
God of Israel reigns! (Isaiah 52:7 NLT)

Jesus spoke to the people once more and said, "I am the light of the
world. If you follow me, you won't have to walk in darkness, because you
will have the light that leads to life."
(John 8:12 NLT)

"You are the light of the world. A city set on a hill cannot be hidden."
(Matt. 5:14 NLT)

———————— ** ————————

Love Divine

Blissful in the vineyard,
drinking the new wine in love with the divine.

Sinful in pinewood.
All is not fine affecting my mood, so I pine for my love divine.

Refine the prodigal, that is me!
free from a fine 'cause it was paid on a tree.

Bind me to the divine. A love bond where we forever entwine.

Pexel

The Sky's the Limit
**

Ignoring crucial
matters is as
swimming in
shallow waters.
Fear of the advance
is as living within
enemy's borders.

Our mandate is to
delve deeper.
The sky's the limit.
We look to see,
listen to hear,
and read to understand.
When we are done,
we act to accomplish.

A special people,
with gifts and
potential.
Born with plenty
we are determined
to utilise all and
return to dust empty.

———— ** ————

The Beautifier

At Beautiful Gate,
as lame ones on the floor,
in a pitiful state
we have hope galore.

The length of restriction
we know not,
the time of our healing, a
clue we have not,
but with God as a forte,
we fear not.

Shaken but not crushed,
Our faith is "the substance
of things hoped for the evidence
of things not seen"[1].

When the set time comes,
substance of things are dreams
realised, evidence of things are
healings attained, for the restorer
arises as the sun that beams it's
smile across the sky
and says "I make everything
beautiful in my time'"[2]

Scriptural inspiration: Acts 3, Quotes: (1) Heb.11: 1 (KJV)
(2) paraphrased Ecc. 3:11 (ERV)

Blessings

A life was sacrificed to pay the price,
so a curse without a cause will not alight.

Streams of sorrow no more your portion,
but rivers of laughter are for your immersion.

Your blocked dam becomes a fountain of living
water and your barren terrain is now a
green pasture.

The blessings offered are your predestined right,
so that you can flourish daily and do exploits
with all your might.

Scriptural inspiration: Gal 3:13, Prov. 26:2, John 15:12-18

———— ** ————

The Journey

Truth at the wheel.
Knowledge a Satnav,
navigates.
Clarity of view is real.
Destination set out,
invigorates.

Purposeful with
Faithful and True, the rider.
Fruitful, we do not tire.

Rocky paths, mishaps
and deliberate traps
are no match for
Living Word, a liberation
map that avoids fearful
dead ends and leads to
joyful glorious ends.

______________**______________

The Holy Child's Tale

The Word is a light unto their pathway.
The Spirit flows out of their belly waterway.

Steps anoint paths all around.
Speech ignite holy fire to reclaim the enemy's ground.

Arms embrace the needy, give to the
hungry and feet dance to the Almighty.

This is the Holy Child's tale,
never stale. A story to the
glory of God Almighty.

Pure & True

Pure, Pure, Pure
are the words of the Lord.
Sweet as honeycomb to hearts
yielded and ready for integrity.

True, True, True
are the words of the Lord
Fragranced with the scent of grace
that only seekers of truth can appreciate.

__________ ** __________

The Overcomer

The Master I have
is my mentor and
determines my gain.
Setbacks are all in vain.

The Saviour I have
is my appraiser
and takes on my pain.
Attempts to derail me
are all in vain.

The Protector I have,
my Master and Saviour,
sanctifies and preserves
my soul.
By Him I overcome and
I'm made whole.

Pexel

Abandoned in Worship

All honour
glory,
splendour,
majesty
we ascribe to Him who
sits on the throne.

In complete abandon,
with vigour hot as a rod,
fervour as children of God
we worship Him who
sits on the throne.

Resting under His gaze,
we are amazed at His
favour and grace.

———— ** ————

Redeemed
**

Blood spilled,
redemption fulfilled.

Blood bought,
life well-wrought.

Death defeated,
birth repeated.

Death swallowed,
victory followed.

Clean slate,
is now my fate.

______ ** ______

A Virtuous Plea
**

Righteousness rise upon me
as the sun that I may be healed.
Goodness and mercy follow me
daily, is my humble plea.

Faithfulness be my ride to guide
each day, so that success is the sure
outcome in my life everyday.

__________ ** __________

The Banquet

A Banquet is ready.
The Master sends His Servant
to invite guests with a voice to proclaim:

The narrow way, a gate
of access to eternal bliss,
is the way of success
that's a child of God's fate.

The broad way, a gate of
access to eternal distress
is a way of sadness,
that's a route not to take,
dear mate.

Many heard the call,
but stayed clad in old
attires, lied and made
excuses, siding with
humanity's fall.

A Banquet is ready.
A new call out to guests by
the Servant with his aids:
"We search highways and
byways for the poor, maim,
blind and lame."

A needy people with humility
void of airs and graces
receive the joys and savouries of the Master's house.
His Banquet guests forever
in eternal bliss.
"Many are called but few are chosen..." (Matthew 22:14)

Scriptural inspiration: Luke 14:15:24, Matthew 22:1-14

In Jesus, I Am Victorious
_*_

Arise and praise He who is worthy and for Him
raise your hands in adoration.

Acclaim and proclaim what He has done and by Him
reclaim your possession.

Confront the affront to your faith,
and declare by Jesus you are victorious.

Arise, raise hands without restraint.
Acclaim, reclaim without growing faint.

Today, tomorrow and always proclaim
"In Jesus, I am victorious"

———— ** ————

Peace Reign

Peace reign in my stead.
My heart I daily leave ajar
for your calming essence
that I may be a fragrance,
a channel of rest
in the realm of a soothing fest,
this world knowest not.

Peace come hither,
reign in my stead.

Commission in Motion
**

As a locomotive fueled with godly motives,
they are set in motion for God's commission.

Beautified feet to bring good news
to ears ready for the sweet
Gospel message void of bad news.

Holy hands raised in praise.
Living a life that is traced to him witness is
borne in every act and phrase.

Bended knees in prayer for the afflicted to
overcome the destroyer and be comforted.

Hands as God's to comfort, His touch to caress.
Voice as God's to uplift and ears as His to listen.

How beautiful upon the mountains
Are the feet of him who brings good news,
Who proclaims peace,
Who brings glad tidings of good *things,*
Who proclaims salvation,
Who says to Zion,
"Your God reigns!" (Isaiah 52:7 NKJV)

[18] And Jesus came and spoke to them, saying, "All authority has been given to Me in heaven and on earth. [19] Go therefore and make disciples of all the nations, baptizing them in the name of the Father and of the Son and of the Holy Spirit, [20] teaching them to observe all things that I have commanded you; and lo, I am with you always, *even* to the end of the age." Amen. (Matthew 28:18-20 NKJV)

State of the Heart
**

A widow gave her mite,
small it was in the offertory,
but much it was in God's sight
'cause it was out of her poverty.

Not what you give,
nor the amount you offer
but your motive and manner
is what pleases God the Father.

Hannah was relentless
in praying for a child.
God took away her barrenness,
as soon as she promised Him her child.

Not what you pray,
nor the length of your prayer
but your motive and manner
will move the hand of your Heavenly Father.

" I, the LORD, have spoken! "I will bless those who have humble
and contrite hearts, who tremble at my word.[1]"

Scriptural inspiration: Isa. 57:16-17 Quote (1) Is.66:2

More

More of you LORD
is what I seek day and night,
for revelation and insight.

I long to dwell where you are always,
to see your power in every way.
Show me your face, today and always.

More of you LORD
is what I seek morning to evening
for renewal and healing.

I desire to know you always,
to hear your voice everyday.
Show me your glory, forever I pray.

More of you, LORD.

Jesus for Me Has Done It All

___*___

There is nothing I cannot do
'cause Jesus for me has done it all.

When fear shows its head
to make me tremble in my stead,
I shall raise my hands in praise
and proclaim the gospel instead.

When fear at the door knocks
with morbid echoes as it's sound
in moments when my life boat
rocks, I shall tune in to the joy
bells of Jesus, the Rock of Salvation.

_________**_________

In This Season

In this season of festivity,
where shopping is in abundance,
let love spill and share with those in lack to
make them feel relevant.

In this season of nativity,
where carol singing is in abundance,
let minds be still and focus on Christ as Saviour,
the reason for this season of Joyance.

The angel Gabriel said of Mary to Joseph "She will bear a Son;
and you shall call His name Jesus, for He will save His people from
their sins." (Matt.1:21)

———— ** ————

If but for the Birth of Jesus Christ…

If but for the birth of Jesus Christ, where would we be?
Knowing him is the greatest thing that happened to us,
his Saints we will always be.

When Christ our Saviour was born, the light in our lives, God
planned to turn on. No more slaves to sin are we, but now among
the chosen few.

God in Christ is faithful it is true, always ready for men to renew.
As friends of Christ his mysteries to us he imparts,
not only for us to flourish but that we will with zeal, the gospel to
impart. To seal many in Christ and soften hardened hearts.

Scriptural inspiration: John 1:1-5, John 14:11-14, Isaiah 9:6-7
John 15:14-16

All Unto Yah!
**

One says "Your self denial
wins trophies of appraisal".

I say "It's all for Yah!"

Another says "Your self sacrifice
breaks the pride edifice".

I say "All glory to Yah!"

Truly Free!
**

By whom are you free,
redeemed for all to see,
walking on the narrow road of divine liberty?
"..if the Son sets you free, you are truly free"

I am free!

Saved by him who died on the tree.
Enjoying abundant life and abiding in the shadow of the
Almighty.

I am truly free!

Scriptural inspiration: Quote: John 8:36 NLT

———— ** ————

I Surrender

My life is yours, your glory to impart.

I surrender my life withholding nothing. Even in the midst of
turmoil & strife, I surrender everything.

My hands are yours, your works to perform. My feet are yours,
your strides to take.

I give my life to you, withholding nothing. Even in the midst of
storms without delay, I surrender everything.

My life is yours, your glory to impart.

For My Sake
— * —

Debased,
subject to the enemy's game.
Distressed,
though no one could tame.
Defaced,
marred and lacking fame.
Disgraced,
on the Cross of shame.

By His grace,
I shall never be the same.

**

Yah: A God of all, above all

Yah is awesome.
Awe-inspiring to all.
Accepting of all.

Yah is worthy of honour.
Honour rendered to
Him above all.
Lifted up above all.

Awesome God of all.
Honoured above all.

Listen...
Do you hear that still small
voice.
The voice like a whisper in your
ear, that
voice pleading,
reaching out,
tagging at your heart strings,
coaxing you to draw near,
saying "never give up,
always persevere and receive
hope, peace and joy of your
God, Yah
who is always near."
Listen...

For more information:
Bearwitness-Forerunner Ministries International

Email: bearwitnessforerunner88@gmail.com